WARGAMES SERIES

EDITOR: TERENCE WISE

GW00645599

THE CAMPAIGN OF
LEIPZIG 1813

Text by JEFF PARKER

Colour plates arranged by PETER GILDER

Colour map by CHRISTINE HOWES

OSPREY PUBLISHING LONDON

Published in 1979 by
Osprey Publishing Ltd
Member company of the George Philip Group
12–14 Long Acre, London WC2E 9LP
© Copyright 1979 Osprey Publishing Ltd

ISBN 0 85045 338 0

Filmset in United Kingdom
Printed in Hong Kong

The bridge at Pfaffendorf. (This, and all other
vignettes of landscape and architecture, are courtesy
David Golden.)

Introduction

On 5 December 1812 Napoleon abandoned the
remnants of his *Grande Armée* on its disastrous
retreat from Moscow and returned to Paris to
face the greatest crisis of his career. The problems
he had to overcome to maintain his influence and
his Empire were enormous. Russia looked as if
she intended to carry the war into Europe, and
was doing all in her power to form an alliance
with Prussia. Austria, while outwardly presenting
a show of neutrality, was only waiting for an
opportune moment to strike; and the German
states showed all the signs of being on the verge
of revolt. A Swedish force of 27,000 men had
landed in Pomerania to reclaim that province and,
far away in Spain, the Anglo-Portuguese army was
meeting with success in its campaign of liberation.

These difficulties would have broken the will of
most men, but Napoleon had begun raising a new
army even before he left Russia. France still had
considerable resources of manpower to draw
upon, even if not of the highest quality. New
battalions were formed about cadres of veterans
from Spain, Italy and Russia. Retired officers
were recalled and NCOs promoted to provide the
junior leadership. Intake to the training depots
was staggered, and the newly-trained recruits

marched to the front in 'provisional regiments', a
system made necessary by the need to keep
stragglers to a minimum, and as a safeguard
against the bands of Cossacks who infested the
French lines of communication throughout the
campaign.

By calling up conscripts ahead of time, as well
as men passed over in earlier levies, and by
transferring young men from the National Guard
to the regular army, sufficient men were found to
form a field army of 250,000 men, and to replace
losses and furnish garrisons to the tune of
another 100,000.

Napoleon's first plan for the recovery of his
fortunes envisioned a drive on Danzig, collecting
reinforcements from the Rhine Confederation *en
route*. His presence in the area would quell
unrest in Germany, and his arrival at Danzig
would relieve the Vistula garrisons and place him
in a position to descend on the Russian rear.
One good victory would discourage Russia and
force Austria into a more convincing attitude of
neutrality. The entry of Prussia into the war
caused a postponement of this scheme, but it was
never entirely abandoned.

While the new army was being raised, Eugène

The Leipzig Campaign 1813

de Beauharnais was entrusted with the task of holding back the Russians. Murat gave over command of what was left of the *Grande Armée* to Eugène at Posen in East Prussia. The least damaged part of the army, the corps on either wing, had comprised 20,000 Prussians under Yorck in the north, and 29,000 Austrians under Schwarzenberg in the south. Yorck defected to the Russians on 30 December 1812 and commenced a period of reorganization at Königsberg. The Austrians did not conclude a formal arrangement, but instead withdrew peacefully to Galicia, carrying Poniatowski's 8,000 Polish troops with them. Danzig held a garrison of 30,000 Frenchmen, and there were another 20,000 in the remaining Vistula fortresses. Eugène was left with a force of 12,000 infantry and 2,000 cavalry, but by the end of March this had been increased to 62,000 altogether.

Opposed to him were, from right to left, Wittgenstein with 30,000 Russians covering Danzig, Admiral Chichagov's 20,000 advancing on Thorn and Miloradovich, plus 30,000 more watching Schwarzenberg's retirement. Another 20,000 reinforcements were coming up to Warsaw. Blücher was raising a Prussian corps at Breslau in Silesia and refusing to submit these men to Eugène's orders. Eugène must have been overwhelmed but for the Russians' need of rest and reorganization. While they waited along the Vistula, Wittgenstein organized three bodies of Cossacks, each 1,500 strong, to raid behind the enemy lines. These 'free corps', while not strategically important, caused much damage to the French throughout the campaign.

The Russians resumed their advance in early February and towards the end of March Eugène had been pushed back to the Elbe between Magdeburg and Dresden. Behind him, at Erfurt, the new army was almost ready. Napoleon left Paris on 15 April to begin his campaign.

The Commanders

Napoleon I, Emperor of the French (1769–1821)
It is generally recognized that Napoleon reached the peak of his powers in 1806. His talents declined after this date, although his ambition, personal magnetism and ability to cope with enormous workloads were undiminished. His fall has been ascribed to any number of things, but at the heart of the matter lay his character. Ambition and, indeed, ability made him the most thorough of autocrats. With few exceptions, government ministers and army commanders alike were discouraged from exercising initiative and consequently the highest posts in his service were filled by men unfitted for originality of thought and independence of action. As the Empire expanded, this extreme centralization proved its own undoing. In 1813, while Napoleon was winning on one battlefield, his subordinates were losing elsewhere. His health, too, was suffering, and he was prone to long periods of lethargy, particularly after a battle. Nevertheless, his mere presence on a battlefield remained a powerful inducement to victory.

Prince Ludwig Adolf Wittgenstein (1768–1842)
Wittgenstein first came to prominence in the 1812 campaign. He succeeded Kutusov as Commander-in-Chief of the Russian army when the latter died on 16 April 1813, but excessive interference by the Czar forced his resignation after the battle of Lützen.

Prince Michael Bogdanovich Barclay de Tolly (1761–1818)
Wittgenstein was replaced at the end of May by Barclay, who thus returned to the post which he had previously lost to Kutusov after Borodino. He remained C-in-C for the remainder of the campaign. Neither of these Russian commanders were of the same calibre as Kutusov.

Field-Marshal Gebhard Leberecht von Blücher (1742–1819)
Blücher was given command of the Prussian army on 28 February 1813. He had been a professional soldier since the age of sixteen. In 1813 he was

Wachau

seventy-one and still leading cavalry charges. Lacking in formal education, fond of drinking and gambling, he still possessed the absolute trust of his soldiers. He was a shrewd judge of men, and sufficiently aware of his own shortcomings to ensure that his chiefs-of-staff had whatever qualities he himself lacked. His impetuosity made an excellent foil for the caution of his allies. He was prone to ill health and even bouts of insanity during periods of forced inactivity.

Prince Karl Philipp von Schwarzenberg (1771–1820)
Five days after Austria's declaration of war in August, Prince Schwarzenberg was made Generalissimo of the Allied armies, superseding Barclay. He was an experienced soldier and an able diplomat. This was an important quality in an affair involving multi-national forces, the more so since his plans were continually subjected to interference by the Prussian and Russian monarchs as well as by his own Emperor, Francis. His difficulties were acknowledged even by Blücher, a fierce critic of Schwarzenberg's over-cautious approach.

Jean Baptiste Bernadotte (1763–1844)
Bernadotte was a complex character with a reputation as an opportunist and as a humanitarian. In 1813 he had seen over thirty years of military service and three years before had been elected Crown Prince Karl Johan of Sweden. He was always a difficult subordinate, and he deservedly earned Napoleon's mistrust. In the early days of the Consulate he was an intractable opponent of Napoleon, and it is likely that he was made a Marshal of the Empire more as a bribe than as a reward for his services.

A French water waggon of the period. (Richard Scollins)

The Armies

The French Army

Napoleon's new army did not compare well with the instrument of earlier years. The conscripts were young and suffered cruelly from the rigours of campaigning. A forced march would leave many of them strewn along the route to be rounded up later by special patrols. Many of them only received musket training on the march to the front. Part of the blame for the inconclusiveness of most of the battles of the campaign can be laid to the lack of energy of the French soldiers for the all-important pursuit after victory.

The officers at middle and higher levels were as good as ever, but battle losses from these ranks could not easily be replaced. At the start of the campaign there was a good ratio of one officer to thirty or forty men, but the situation grew worse later in the year with the arrival of thousands of new recruits. Even with these drawbacks the infantry showed traditional courage and élan, especially when supported by the artillery, which remained excellent.

The cavalry gave most cause for concern. Until the beginning of May the army had only 11,000 French and 4,000 allied cavalry. After this date the newly-trained recruits began to arrive, but they were of very inferior quality. This want of good cavalry affected much of Napoleon's planning. The task of the cavalry off the battlefield was to procure intelligence and to prevent the enemy from doing the same. Napoleon liked to manoeuvre his army behind an impenetrable screen of cavalry so that the enemy could not know where and in what strength the blow would fall. In 1805, before the battle of Austerlitz, six cavalry divisions effectively screened about 150 miles of front.

The lines along which the French army was organized remained unchanged. It was a tried and tested system which combined the flexibility needed to meet changing circumstances with the degree of permanency necessary for the development of good order and an *esprit de corps*. The largest formation within the army was the corps which was itself a miniature army of all arms. A corps could number as few as 10,000 or as many as 30,000 men depending on the task it had to perform. Once constituted it usually remained intact throughout a campaign, although detachments might be taken from or added to it temporarily as circumstances required. A typical corps would have three divisions of infantry and a division of light cavalry. Divisional strengths varied enormously under campaign conditions. Each division had a company (or battery) of artillery, foot for the infantry and horse for the cavalry, and there would be a corps reserve of two foot artillery companies. Each corps had its own complement of engineers, quartermasters, and so on.

All of the heavy cavalry was massed in cavalry corps which almost invariably had two divisions of two brigades. The brigades in turn were comprised of two regiments. Where an infantry regiment might have between two and six battalions, each about 600 strong under campaign conditions and not always serving on the same front, the heavy cavalry always had three, and light cavalry regiments four squadrons, each perhaps 150 strong.

The speed with which Napoleon's army moved contributed greatly to success. Nothing as cumbersome as supply trains were to hamper the troops while they marched. Four days' rations were issued to each man, but it was expected that they would continue an early tradition of living off the land, saving the rations until a battle was imminent and foraging unsafe. Often only a victory enabled the men to eat and replenish their

ammunition supplies. Napoleon normally expected no more from his troops than ten or twelve miles a day but, when occasion demanded, they could manage thirty-five or even close to fifty miles a day for short periods. This kind of effort took its toll of men, especially among the young recruits of 1813.

The Russian Army

The idea of the army corps along French lines was entirely missed by the Allied commanders. Semi-permanent formations did exist, but in most cases they were hardly a balanced force of all arms. There was a tendency to dissipate the cavalry and artillery among the brigades and divisions so that neither arm could be concentrated for a decisive blow in true Napoleonic style.

The Russian army was the exception, for in 1812 it was reorganized into permanent infantry and cavalry corps. The infantry corps had no organic cavalry. Each infantry corps had two divisions with three brigades in each, one brigade being composed of Jäger regiments. The brigades were formed from two regiments each of two battalions.

Impression of the battle of Lützen, 2 May 1813, with Napoleon and his staff in left foreground.

There were two divisions of five cuirassier regiments and eight other divisions of mixed heavy and light cavalry. These usually had four dragoon and two hussar or ulan regiments organized in three brigades, two heavy and one light. The cuirassiers were organized in two brigades. Russian cavalry regiments had five squadrons serving in the field.

The artillery of the period was very good and was usually deployed in massed batteries. There does not seem to have been any permanent allocation of artillery to the corps. The positioning of the guns on the day of battle was made the responsibility of some convenient officer. This will serve as a nice example of how the special characteristics of the different armies can be reflected in a wargame. Normally there will be a supreme commander with a number of subordinate players controlling the corps or a section of the line. If, in the case of the Russians, one player is given sole responsibility for the artillery, then the situation will approach historical reality with every corps commander bleating for artillery

The road to Stötteritz

support and none of them getting complete satisfaction!

One of the umpire's greatest responsibilities is to see that the armies are organized and fought as were their real life counterparts. Another example which can be drawn from the Russian command system is the unfortunate situation of the Commander-in-Chief. He frequently had at his elbow a Czar who fancied himself as something of a general and who too often listened to the opinions of the C-inC's jealous rivals. A cunning umpire will make the most of this state of affairs in his efforts to direct the campaign in a reasonably accurate fashion. By now it will be clear that the umpire has a difficult task, but it is a rewarding one and it can be eased in small ways. One of these is the use of battle rules (as opposed to campaign rules) which take account of national characteristics. Rules of this kind are available commercially, as indeed are basic campaign rules.

The Russians were known to march faster than the French on occasion. They frequently lived off the land from necessity, much to the annoyance of the ally whose territory they were on. It was their policy when retreating to carry off or destroy anything that might be of use to the enemy, a source of much distress to the French. This ability for rapid movement was nullified, however, by long periods of inactivity during which dissenting commanders wrangled over the future course of action.

The endurance of the Russian soldier is legendary, both on the march and on the battlefield. The army that fought in 1813 was essentially the same as that which faced Napoleon the previous year. True, the regiments were down to

half strength and replacements had to be found from new recruits, but this was still a better state of affairs than was Napoleon's. It cannot be said that the Russian command was characterized by bold, imaginative strokes of strategy or tactics, but the officers knew the qualities of their men and how best to use them. Tenacity and steadiness may not always win battles but they often help to avoid a defeat.

The Prussian Army

The reconstituted Prussian army had many praiseworthy qualities. Its soldiers came from a race with an established military tradition. Discipline continued to be harsh, but a genuine feeling of nationalism was being created which encouraged the soldiers to fight more willingly. This attitude was fostered by the iniquities of the French occupying forces in the previous years. The net result was that the organization became more flexible and setbacks were less likely to bring about a total collapse than had been the case in 1806–07. Indeed, Marshal Blücher's battle record shows many more defeats than victories; but his ability to withdraw his men, re-form and be ready for battle again in a very short time shows that his army had grasped what Napoleonic warfare was all about. This idea is reinforced by the vigorous pursuit of the enemy which the Prussians managed on the occasions when victory was theirs. The troops combined something of the best of both French and Russian armies. They could defend stubbornly, yet attack with great élan. In the struggle for villages which characterized the battles of the campaign, the fighting in the Prussian sectors of the line was invariably the most vicious.

A Prussian corps was a mixture of all arms. There were no separate cavalry corps and no divisions as in other armies. A corps commander had to deal directly with his brigade officers. Each corps consisted of four infantry brigades of three regiments, and two or three cavalry brigades. These normally had three, but sometimes as many as five regiments. Infantry regiments had one fusilier and two musketeer battalions, while the cavalry regiments all had four squadrons.

Impression of the battle of Dresden, 26 August 1813.

As for the artillery, the general aim was to provide each brigade with a foot or horse battery according to type, and to have a couple of foot and one horse battery as corps reserve. Most of the Prussian artillery was lost in 1806 and so much of the artillery in use in 1813 was of British origin.

The Austrian Army

One early author described the Austrians as being 'animated by the hope of avoiding defeat, rather than by . . . determination and assurance of victory'. This same author describes the Austrian soldier as slow by nature. The poor Austrians faced the 1813 campaign with few traditions of victory behind them, and still clinging to outmoded ideas of strategy and tactics. The whole army moved terribly slowly, except in retreat. This ponderous character did have an advantage in that a beaten Austrian army did not disintegrate as rapidly as some others.

In the 1813 campaign the Austrian corps appear to have a fixed number of three infantry divisions, but accounts of earlier campaigns show a more flexible approach. Even with a fixed number of divisions the Austrian corps varied in strength because a division could have two to four brigades each of four or five two-battalion regiments (in

common with all other armies a weak depot battalion also existed to absorb and train new recruits). Each corps had a brigade of cavalry attached, but the heavy cavalry was used to form reserve divisions.

The artillery was very poor. The lighter gun batteries were assigned one to every two infantry regiments, while a heavy battery was allocated to each division. Cavalry brigades were given a horse artillery battery, but these were hardly more mobile than the foot artillery.

One interesting innovation for the Leipzig campaign was the formation of three light divisions. These each had four battalions of Jägers, a few squadrons of light cavalry and a horse battery. Austrian Jägers were of fairly good quality, but were never employed in numbers equal to the French voltigeurs.

The Swedish Army

The Swedes only contributed a single corps of three divisions to the campaign, along with a number of cavalry regiments. The troops were good and very eager to fight. Swedish divisions had three brigades of five or six battalions with a couple of companies of light infantry and a similar number of light cavalry squadrons. The artillery had been weak, but Bernadotte worked to

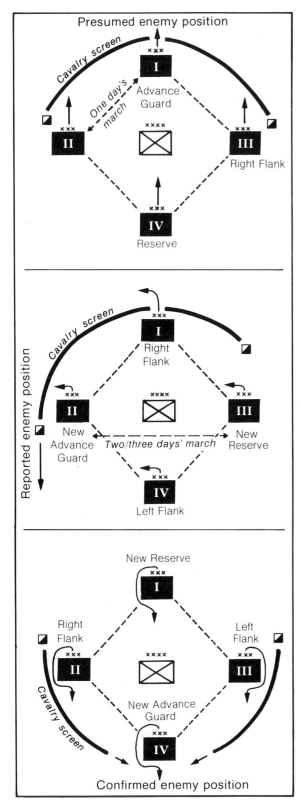

The French *Bataillon Carré* system of manoeuvre: schematic diagram, after Chandler.

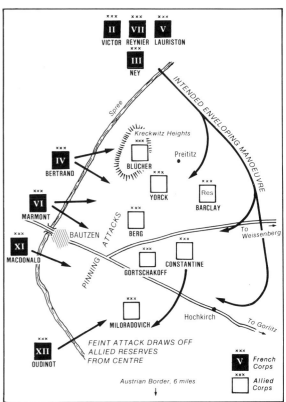

Schematic diagram, not to scale, of the battle of Bautzen, 20–21 May 1813, demonstrating Napoleon's strategic *manoeuvre sur les derrières*.

improve this situation. Resupplying the troops from Sweden proved difficult, and the Swedes found they had to beg, borrow or steal equipment from their allies or enemies.

Strategy and Tactics

Napoleon made it clear that the first objective of any campaign should be the destruction of the opposing armies. Nothing could then prevent the occupation of geographical objectives and the submission of the enemy government. He always sought to bring on a decisive battle, using speed and the unique corps organization to help him.

The system of living off the land meant that speed could be achieved, but it also meant that the corps had to travel along different routes. Napoleon knew that an army strung out on the march must be able to concentrate rapidly when the time for battle came. The movement of every corps was carefully supervised by Napoleon so that, when contact with the enemy was made, they could concentrate by forced marches to gain an advantage. A single corps, being a balanced, all-arms force, was able to fight a defensive battle for a few hours against a force several times its size while this concentration was taking place. There are many examples of enemy commanders attacking a single French corps believing it to be isolated, only to find at the height of the battle that the intended victim was being reinforced while still more troops were appearing on the flanks and in the rear.

When the location and intention of the enemy were unknown, the French commonly adopted the *bataillon carré* formation. This ensured that all were within supporting distance of each other and, more importantly, that the whole army could change its direction of march without disruption as soon as more precise information about the enemy was discovered. The Allies put less thought into their movements and were content to march their armies in two or three long columns.

As soon as the enemy's location was known and his intentions guessed at, Napoleon would begin an outflanking manoeuvre, using cavalry or the terrain to screen the movement. A feint would be made against the enemy's front to draw him deeper into the trap and to pin him long enough for the outflanking manoeuvre to succeed. This *manoeuvre sur les derrières* was usually fatal.

As the battle opens we find the opposing troops

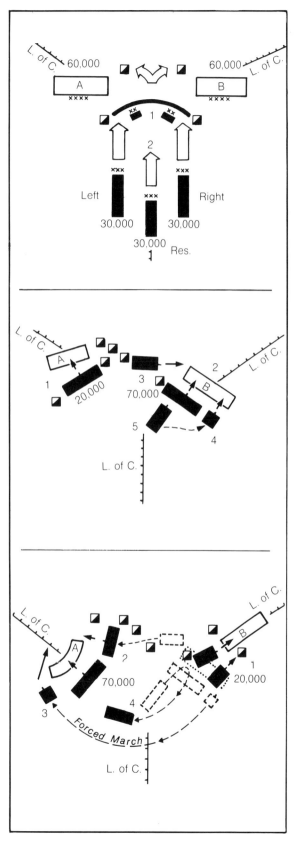

Schematic diagram, after Chandler, showing phases in Napoleon's 'strategy of the central position'. *Phase 1*: the French take the initiative, with (1) cavalry and advanced guard taking central position between enemy forces A and B, and (2) main French force advancing in two wings with a reserve. *Phase 2*: Enemy force B is initial French target. (1) and (2), French wings engage both enemy forces; (3) secondary wing contains enemy force A while sending one division to flank right wing of enemy force B; (4) part of the reserve extends the front of the French right wing; (5) rest of reserve forms the 'mass of decision'. *Phase 3*: Superior French strength now switches to destroy enemy force A. (1) French right wing and cavalry pursue defeated enemy force B from field; (2) detached left wing division returns to parent formation; (3) part of French reserve force-marches to come up on exposed flank of enemy force A; (4) rest of reserve countermarches to repeat its rôle as the 'mass of decision'.

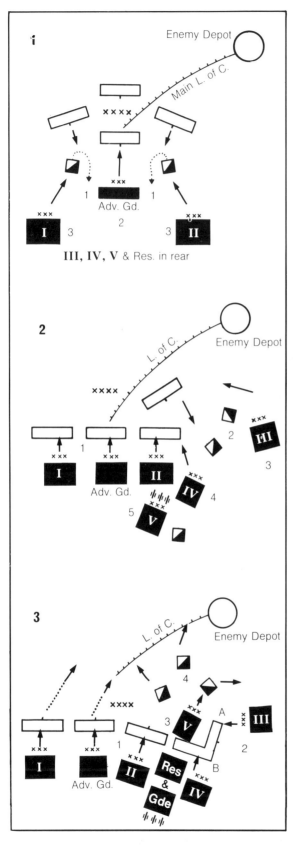

face to face. Napoleon launches assault after assault against the enemy position until the latter has committed all his reserves to positions along the hard-pressed line. Suddenly a new French force appears on a flank and troops must be taken from somewhere out of the line to meet this threat, creating a weak point at which Napoleon threw his own reserves, kept back, often in a concealed position, until this very moment. Napoleon's genius made it possible for the out-flanking force to appear only after the enemy's reserves were committed and for his own reserves to be positioned exactly where the enemy would weaken his line to meet the new threat. The victories won in this way became less impressive with the passage of time. Napoleon's enemies eventually understood the process themselves, but it seems as if his own subordinates never did, and in 1813 they let him down too often by their failure to grasp what was required of them.

The Campaign

The Russian army at the beginning of 1813 numbered 70,000 infantry, 30,000 cavalry and about 700 guns. By the end of April this force had increased to 87,000 infantry and 45,000 cavalry with over 1,000 guns. The Prussians declared war on 16 March, twelve days after Eugène abandoned Berlin. Only King Frederick William's timidity prevented an earlier declaration. The

Schematic diagram, after Chandler, of Napoleon's basic battle plan. *Phase 1*: Contact and pinning attack: **(1) cavalry screen reports contact; (2) Advance guard engages at once; (3) nearest French corps move up to extend front, pulling in more enemy troops.** *Phase 2*: **French moves are covered by a battle of attrition: (1) more enemy troops drawn into battle by frontal attack; cavalry screen (2) conceals enveloping force (3) moving to attack enemy flank adjacent to his lines of communication; (4) reinforcement of front attracts last enemy reserves; (5) 'mass of decision' masses behind French right flank.** *Phase 3*: **Envelopment, breakthrough, and pursuit: (1) frontal attacks continue to pin enemy; (2) enveloping attack forces enemy to weaken his left to form new line A–B; (3) 'mass of decision', preceded by artillery bombardment, penetrates weakened enemy sector; (4) light cavalry follows through gap and commences pursuit.**

terms imposed on Prussia after 1806 limited her army to a strength of 42,000. At the end of 1812 she had only 33,000 men under arms: 20,000 with Yorck at Königsberg, the rest in Silesia. A French call for more troops gave an excuse for calling up the reservists and raising new recruits. By the outbreak of war, an excellent army of 56,000 men with 200 guns could be fielded, with a similar number of half-trained recruits available. On 17 March a Royal Decree brought the Landwehr into being, so providing a future reserve of 100,000 infantry and 12,000 cavalry.

Napoleon's strength was also increasing. At the end of April, Eugène's Army of the Elbe was concentrated behind the lower Saale below Naumberg. He had the completed corps of Macdonald and Lauriston, Latour-Maubourg's cavalry corps, two infantry divisions under Victor (6,000) and Durutte (4,500), which were destined to form the basis of II and VII Corps, and a Guard division (3,500). Napoleon's Army of the Main was on the upper Saale, above Naumberg. It comprised the corps of Ney, Marmont, Bertrand, Oudinot and the infantry and cavalry of the Guard. Davout had 20,000 men on the lower Elbe, where he was watched from Pomerania by Bernadotte's Swedes.

The rest of the Allies were disposed as follows: about Dessau, facing Eugène, was Wittgenstein's command comprising the corps of Bülow, Yorck, Kleist and Berg. Blücher's command was to the south of Leipzig and was made up of his own corps and that of Winzingerode. The Russian reserves under Tormassov and Miloradovich were marching from Dresden. These two were under the Czar's direction, since they refused to serve under Wittgenstein, to whom they were both senior. Barclay was marching from the successful seige of Thorn. Spandau had also fallen, but Stettin and Danzig were still in French hands. Torgau was being held by Theilmann's Saxons, under orders from the king of Saxony to remain neutral.

The strengths of the various corps of both sides at this time are given in a table at the end of the book.

While Napoleon concentrated his forces along the Saale, the Allies were having trouble making decisions. The first plan envisaged Wittgenstein standing at Leipzig with Blücher to the south of him at Altenburg, while further south still, on the extreme left, Miloradovich and Tormassov with the Reserve and Guard Corps moved through Chemnitz (present-day Karl Marx Stadt) and Zwickau. They believed it would be several weeks before Napoleon was ready to move, and that when he did it would be with the Army of the Main towards Leipzig. If this happened Blücher, Miloradovich and Tormassov would be in an excellent position to attack his right flank from the south. When it became apparent that Napoleon was going to move sooner than expected, the Allies were once again thrown into confusion.

After proposal and counter-proposal it was decided to concentrate at Leipzig and to offer a head-on battle east of that town, which would mean falling back slightly. When Alexander heard of these arrangements (he was away visiting his sister) he sent immediate orders to cancel them. By this time the French had appeared at Weissenfels just to the west of Leipzig, and so it was decided that the Allies should assemble between Leipzig and Altenburg and attack Napoleon's right flank through Lützen. This was more or less a return to the first plan.

The Allies were right in believing that Napoleon would attack through Leipzig, but his move was based on lack of information of the enemy's true position, caused by a want of cavalry. Napoleon thought the Allies were much further to the south-east, towards Dresden. His intention was to pass through Leipzig around their right flank and to launch an attack from the rear, with his front towards France, as at Jena and Auerstadt in 1806. The French alone could risk this manoeuvre because of their speed and their lack of dependence, for a short time at least, on supply trains. A defeat would be disastrous; but the French outnumbered the Allies, and Napoleon himself commanded—defeat was not likely. A *manoeuvre sur les derrières* was called for in this instance by the need to force a decisive battle. If, after appreciating Napoleon's real strength, the Allies were threatened only from the front, they would merely fall back and nothing would be achieved. Napoleon had learned that the Russians were masters at that game.

The French began to move on 1 May. This time it was faulty intelligence on the part of the Allies which created false optimism. They imagined the French to be strung out in a long column on the road from Weissenfels to Leipzig with only a weak force covering the right flank to the south of Lützen. It was here that the Allies intended to strike, cutting the French column in half and then destroying the part that had already passed through Lützen.

In fact, the point they were about to attack held the strongest corps in the Army of the Main, Ney's III Corps. There were three divisions about Lützen, and two more in the group of villages to the south. The corps of Marmont and Bertrand were within supporting distance to the west, and the Guard was approaching from Weissenfels. It seems that Napoleon was expecting, or perhaps just hoping, that the Allies would attack where they did. His first arrangements allowed for the corps of Lauriston and Bertrand to be positioned to take part in the battle. Ney's corps had only 45,000 men, but within three hours he could have been supported by another 50,000 and three hours later by 45,000 more, who would have appeared on the enemy's flank and rear. Ney was instructed to throw out reconnaissances in the expected direction of the Allies' approach, but this he failed to do. He knew nothing of the Allies' movements until they attacked. Meanwhile Napoleon, hearing nothing from Ney, assumed that there would be no attack and directed Lauriston and Macdonald elsewhere. Macdonald eventually managed to reach the battlefield but Lauriston did not.

The Battle of Lützen
2 May 1813

The Allies approached Ney's position completely unnoticed. Blücher's corps was in two columns with Yorck behind the left and Berg behind the right column. The Russian heavy artillery was with him. A brigade from Winzingerode's corps was left to guard the line of retreat while the rest covered Blücher's right. Miloradovich and the Reserve corps were sent to Zeitz to guard against a possible outflanking movement down the Naumburg-Zeitz road. This body served no useful purpose in the battle. The Russian Guard was to act as reserve on the battlefield, but failed to come up in time. Kleist's corps was left at Leipzig.

When Blücher's men descended from the heights in front of Ney's position, they caught the forward French divisions completely by surprise. If Wittgenstein had allowed Blücher to continue he might have taken all the villages at bayonet point, driving the French out on to the plain where they could have been dealt with by the Allied cavalry. But Wittgenstein, too, was surprised to find 12,000 men where he had expected 2,000, and he halted the advance. The delay enabled the French to sort themselves out and the action opened properly at about noon.

Napoleon was at Leipzig when he heard the cannonade. He had been directing a successful attack by Lauriston's corps on that of Kleist, forcing the latter to abandon the town. He immediately sent orders that Ney was to hold his position with Marmont moving up on his right. Bertrand was to attack the Allied left flank and Macdonald, with Latour-Maubourg's cavalry, the right. Lauriston was ordered to hold Leipzig but to be ready to send two divisions towards Lützen. With these orders issued he set off for the battlefield.

The cannonade that Napoleon heard was a forty-minute one preceding the renewed Allied advance. Blücher continued against the four villages while the cavalry attacked Starsiedel. The cavalry were completely unsuccessful and by 1 p.m. two of Marmont's divisions had arrived enabling Girard's division to go to the aid of Souham. The presence of so many Allied cavalry had forced Marmont to march to Starsiedel in six brigade squares, a point that should be noted by rule-makers who refuse to allow infantry squares any movement at all! Nor was this the first example of the campaign: Napoleon's advance across the Saale had to be conducted in similar fashion because of the superiority of Allied cavalry.

Meanwhile, Blücher's attack on the four villages was a very to-and-fro affair, with the villages continually changing hands as each side fed in

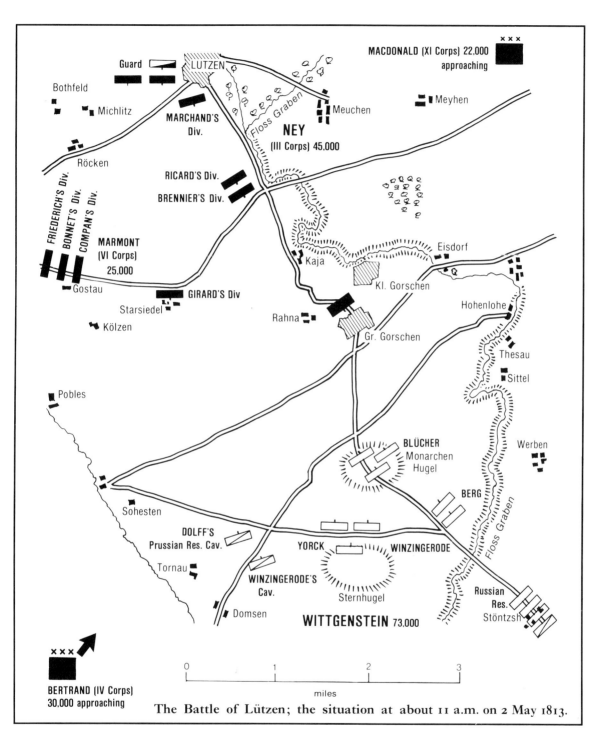

The Battle of Lützen; the situation at about 11 a.m. on 2 May 1813.

more troops. By now both Marmont's and Ney's men were exhausted. Bertrand had halted his advance against Wittgenstein's left on hearing about Miloradovich's corps at Zeitz. There was little that Wittgenstein could do, however. Alexander had delayed the arrival of the Guards and grenadiers of the reserve, intending to lead them in person. By the time they arrived, at about 4 p.m., it was too late.

Napoleon came on to the battlefield at 2.30 p.m. and the situation immediately changed. Morale was revived, Bertrand was ordered to continue his flank attack and the other approaching corps were hurried along. The appearance of these reinforcements at about 6 p.m. forced Wittgenstein to break off the battle and retreat. Darkness and the lack of cavalry prevented the French from pursuing.

Lützen was an unremarkable battle, but it proved that Napoleon's new army could march and fight, and it was undoubtedly a French victory. Estimates of the losses on each side vary greatly, but taking an average figure would give Allied losses as 15,000 and French losses of 20,000, most of whom were from Ney's corps. A few days later stragglers and deserters had reduced the French army by another 15,000. The blame for this is put on the inexperience of the young recruits in living off the land and of coping with the forced marches. Forced marches and battles would continue to produce this drainage of badly-needed men. The situation became so bad that Napoleon had to issue orders for the formation of special patrols to gather up these stragglers.

Ney, after a day's rest to reorganize his battered corps, was sent to relieve the French garrison at Wittenberg. He was joined by Victor's II Corps, Reynier's VII Corps (at present only a single division) and Sebastiani with the 2nd Cavalry Corps and one of Lauriston's divisions. This was a sufficient force with which to wheel the Saxons into line and to present a threat to Berlin. The Saxons in Torgau eventually yielded a division of 9,000 infantry, which were added to Reynier's corps, and four cavalry regiments which went to the 1st Cavalry Corps. The rest of the army marched towards Dresden, with Lauriston on the left providing a link with Ney and keeping an eye open for Kleist's men. Dresden was the obvious place for the Allies to make for, but Napoleon believed they would separate once across the Elbe, the Russians falling back along their line of communications towards Warsaw and the Prussians northwards to protect their capital.

It was true that the Allies were engaged in their customary arguments over future plans, but fortunately the Prussians were induced to disregard Berlin for the time being and to follow the Russians back through Dresden to Bautzen, where Barclay de Tolly was waiting with 13,000 Russian troops fresh from the siege of Thorn.

Bülow's corps, presently at Magdeburg and Halle, would have to suffice for the defence of Berlin.

By 11 May the right of the army under Napoleon's direct command had forced a passage of the Elbe at Dresden; and this marks a convenient place in the account for a small digression. Forced river crossings are not undertaken carelessly, and Napoleon had to select a site at which his guns could command the far bank. Under cover of these a bridgehead could be established and work commenced on the building of a temporary bridge. Now, few wargamers will have access to maps showing terrain features as they existed in Napoleon's time. Nor will many have the resources even to obtain large-scale modern maps of the areas fought over. A lot of imagination is called for in the interpretation of the terrain. The majority of roads shown on a modern map existed in Napoleon's day, if only in a primitive state. The same can be said of bridges. But how are we to judge a suitable site for a battle, or a forced river crossing? The truth is that Napoleon's maps would not have shown such things either. Staff officers would be sent out to make reconnaissances. The umpire can be asked to provide the results of these efforts in the form of sketch maps. He should use his judgement and probably some random system when called upon to produce these. In the case of river crossings, something as simple as a dice throw could decide how many likely spots there are for a successful crossing, and another one could determine how far off they are. The system can be as sophisticated or as simple as you wish. Since river crossings are almost always successful ultimately, you may wish merely to let the dice decide how many hours or days it takes to cross and how many troops are lost in the attempt. Again, the umpire's judgement will be important. All the same, if this situation is wargamed out a few times, it will teach the players a healthy respect for features such as bridges! Incidentally, bridge destruction was not always carried out very effectively — another opportunity for the umpire and his ubiquitous dice.

Returning to the mainstream of the story, we reach the point when, on 16 May, a reconnais-

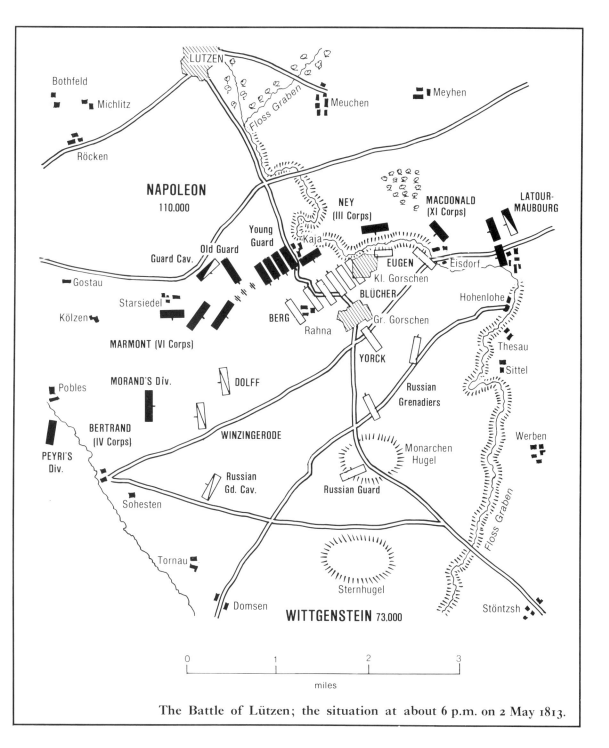

The Battle of Lützen; the situation at about 6 p.m. on 2 May 1813.

sance of the Allied position at Bautzen convinced Napoleon that Wittgenstein intended to offer battle. Instructions were despatched to the corps commanders. Napoleon had been dissatisfied with Eugène's performance to date, and he was now packed off to Italy to raise a corps for the purpose of watching the Austrians in that direction. Ney was given command of the left of the army. The titles of the Army of the Main and the Elbe were now abolished, and the *Grande Armée* was formally reconstituted.

Ney was to allow Victor, Reynier and Sebastiani

to continue towards Berlin, while he himself marched in the direction of Bautzen, picking up Lauriston on the way. Ney's compliance with these orders marked the beginning of a series of misunderstandings which plagued the marshal throughout the remainder of his career. To be fair, Napoleon's orders at this time are not a model of clarity. Whatever the cause, Ney ended up marching his entire force south. Napoleon wanted the Allies to believe that Ney would join the main army in a frontal assault, hence the march towards Bautzen. At the last moment Ney was to swing east and then south again towards Hochkirch in the Allied rear. An expedition, launched on the 19th by Barclay and Yorck in the direction of Ney's force, caused the marshal to imagine he was about to be attacked by the whole of the Allied army. He therefore halted in a defensive position to the north of the real battlefield. Ney's actions throughout this episode show that he failed completely to understand Napoleon's intentions. This state of affairs was to continue during the course of the battle.

The Battle of Bautzen
20–21 May 1813

The Allies were drawn up in prepared positions a little behind the River Spree, facing west. The town of Bautzen and a stretch of the river either side of it were lightly held by Miloradovich, acting as an advance guard. The northern part of the battlefield, where the Allied right stood, comprised an area given over to fish farming. It was a mass of ponds fed by the Spree and traversed by numerous causeways. There were a few areas of high ground which, in the midst of all the muddy ponds, must have seemed particularly attractive. The most important of these was called the Kreckwitz Heights. Barclay de Tolly's men held this wing with Blücher on his left. Further south the ground begins to rise to the wooded heights which extend all the way to the Austrian border, six miles off. The Allies had raised earthworks and redoubts all along the line, but especially on these ridges where their left and centre were positioned. They were convinced that this was where Napoleon's main attack would come. They thought it was his intention to turn

their left and drive them away from Austria. As a consequence most of their strength was located here. In the centre, next to Blücher, was Yorck, with the Russian Guard and reserves, now commanded by Constantine, to the rear of him. The Allied left was held by the corps of Berg and Gortschakov. Why Constantine replaced Tormassov and where exactly Gortschakov sprang from, are questions which must remain unanswered. The appearance and disappearance of Russian commanders is a problem which causes confusion in even the most detailed accounts. We can guess from subsequent events that Winzingerode might have been with Bülow at this time.

Wittgenstein's dispositions played right into Napoleon's hands. His intentions were the complete reverse of what the Allies believed. As we have seen, he planned to pin them with a frontal attack and turn their right with Ney's force, driving them on to the Austrian border. Here they would have to fight their last battle, or violate Austrian neutrality with possibly dire consequences.

Bautzen was to be fought in the well-tried manner described earlier in the section on tactics. Oudinot, Macdonald and Marmont would launch a fierce attack on the Allied front. Bertrand's corps was held back on the left of the main army. When Wittgenstein had committed all his reserves Ney would appear, forcing the Allied general to realign his right to meet the threat. Bertrand's fresh corps would then be hurled at the angle so formed in the enemy's line (always a weak spot) and break through. The battle would be finished. Note that Napoleon still had the Imperial Guard on hand for any unforeseen circumstances.

The delays caused by Ney's blunders determined the Emperor to wage a battle of attrition during 20 May, and to deliver the final stroke the following day when Ney should at last be in position. The attack on the 20th did not commence until the afternoon, but this was deliberate. If the French suffered a serious reverse there would not be enough daylight left for the Allies to make the most of the situation, and Ney's appearance the next day would alter the position entirely. In fact the attack went very well. The French not only got across the Spree and captured

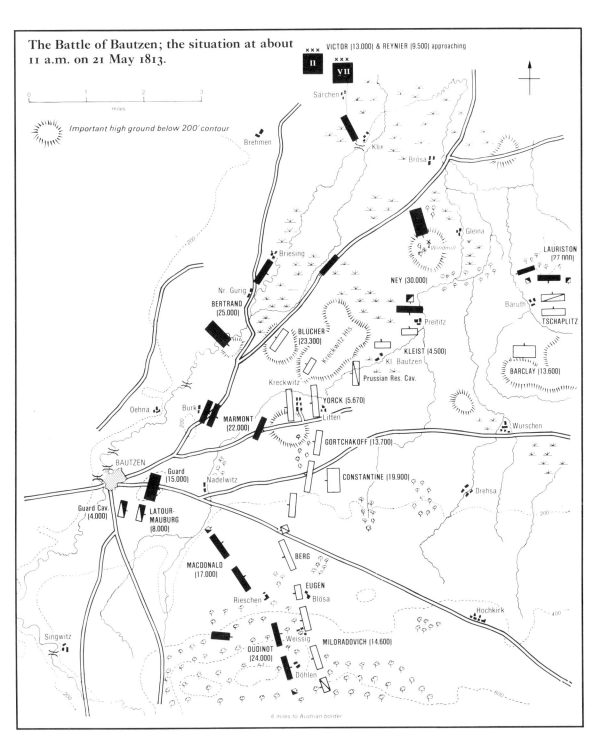

The Battle of Bautzen; the situation at about 11 a.m. on 21 May 1813.

VICTOR (13,000) & REYNIER (9,500) approaching

II

VII

Särchen

Brehmen

Klix

Brösa

0   1   2   3
miles

Important high ground below 200' contour

Gleina

Windmill

LAURISTON (27,000)

Briesing

NEY (30,000)

Baruth

Nr. Gurig

BERTRAND (25,000)

Preititz

TSCHAPLITZ

BLÜCHER (23,300)

Kreckwitz Hts

KLEIST (4,500)

Kl. Bautzen

BARCLAY (13,600)

Kreckwitz

Prussian Res. Cav.

Oehna

Burk

YORCK (5,670)

MARMONT (22,000)

Litten

Wurschen

GORTCHAKOFF (13,700)

BAUTZEN

Guard (15,000)

Nadelwitz

CONSTANTINE (19,900)

Drehsa

Guard Cav. (4,000)

LATOUR-MAUBURG (8,000)

MACDONALD (17,000)

BERG

Rieschen

EUGEN

Blösa

Hochkirk

Singwitz

Weissig

MILORADOVICH (14,600)

OUDINOT (24,000)

Döhlen

6 miles to Austrian border

Bautzen, but Oudinot's efforts on the extreme right of the French line were so vigorous as to convince the Allies that their appraisal of Napoleon's intentions was correct. Ney's movements had been noticed but the size of his force was greatly underestimated.

By the following day Ney was in a position to execute his part in Napoleon's plan. He was to attack Barclay's men and be at the village of Preititz by 11 a.m. Lauriston, meanwhile, was to be on Ney's left and to advance so as to cut the Allied line of retreat eastwards. Ney's corps made

Möckern

good progress and he was in a position to take Preititz and press on. He did not do so because Napoleon's orders said he must be at the village at 11 a.m., and it was yet too early. There was a period of delay during which, no doubt, Ney had a good chance to study his side of the battlefield. He arrived at the conclusion that Blücher's position on the Kreckwitz Heights off to his right held the key to the battle. This was indeed the part of the Allied line that Bertrand's corps was to attack, but it was certainly not Ney's task. If he had continued on through Preititz, Blücher would have been manoeuvred out of his position anyway. All the same, Ney decided to wait for Reynier to come up and then to assault the Heights. He ordered Lauriston to draw in closer to him which was not at all what Napoleon wanted. Lauriston was already late and he actually got no further than Baruth during the day. This, of course, meant that the vital Allied line of retreat remained open. Ney spent the rest of the day battering away at the Kreckwitz Heights and Preititz.

On Napoleon's side of the battlefield things were going more according to plan. Oudinot, Macdonald and Marmont were still pressing their attacks and preventing Wittgenstein from drawing off men to face the threat posed by Ney's appearance. It appears that Wittgenstein divined Napoleon's true intention at some stage but was overruled by the Czar. The Allied line began to bend under the strain of attacks from the west and the north until it formed a right angle with Blücher at the corner. Bertrand's corps was duly launched at this weak spot, and the whole of the Allied right started slowly to give ground. By this time Blücher, still on the Heights, was being attacked from the north-east by Ney and from the west by Bertrand. When he found that Napoleon had called the Guard into line between Bertrand and Marmont, threatening an attack from the south-west, the old Prussian reluctantly agreed to retreat before he became surrounded. With this movement the whole Allied position became untenable. A general retreat was ordered at about 4 p.m. and the columns began to stream east along the roads which Lauriston should have been blocking. Napoleon had gained another incomplete victory. Lack of cavalry and an evening storm again prevented a vigorous pursuit and the Allies were allowed to depart in an orderly manner, leaving 11,000 casualties behind. The French lost twice that number.

The Allies began their easterly retreat amidst the usual bickering over what to do next. Finding his position impossible, Wittgenstein resigned and was replaced by Barclay. The Russians wished to pass right through Silesia into Poland, but the Prussians were unwilling to abandon this part of their territory. It was finally agreed that they should all go south-east to Schweidnitz, which would serve to cover Silesia and keep the armies in touch with Austria. This was not ideal because it presented Napoleon with another chance to turn their right and force them on to the Austrian border. Another two months would pass before Austria was ready to act.

The first leg of the retreat, from Bautzen to Gorlitz, was marked by fierce rearguard actions, not an easy thing to represent in a wargames campaign. The simplest way to deal with the situation is for the umpire to allocate a random number of casualties on both sides for each stretch of road covered by the retreat. These losses will be additional to the regular wastage caused by sickness and desertion.

After passing through Gorlitz the Allies split into two columns travelling by different roads towards Leignitz. Once more the Emperor's hopes of an impending Allied break-up were raised, especially since the troops marching along the northern road were reported to be exclusively Prussian. Ney, still on the left, was ordered to follow along this route with Lauriston and Reynier and to send a force in the direction of Glogau to the north-east. Victor was to make a reconnaissance northwards to see if any of the enemy were headed for Berlin. Marmont, Macdonald, Bertrand and Latour-Maubourg were to travel by the south road. Oudinot, Sebastiani and the Guard were to the rear.

At this point we come across another incident that highlights the inexperience and lack of discipline among the French in 1813. The leading division of Ney's advance, 4,000 infantry under Maison, was strolling through some gently rolling countryside quite unconcerned about such things as putting out scouts. All of a sudden 3,000 Prussian cavalry charged them in flank from a concealed position 400 yards off. The result was not as severe as it might have been, because a village was close at hand into which the French tumbled with remarkable agility. Maison lost a quarter of his men. If this was an isolated incident it could be ignored; but we have already seen Ney's divisions caught off guard at Lützen, and the same thing happened to Bertrand's Italian division during Barclay's brief expedition just before the battle of Bautzen. It certainly happened often enough to be made a minor feature of the campaign. It is one of the 'random events' which an imaginative umpire can create, but, if he values life and limb, he should not push the idea too far!

The Allies reached Schweidnitz on 29 May, but found it unsuitable as a defensive position. Besides, news reached them that the French were at Breslau and threatening to cut them from the Oder. They consequently moved towards that river themselves, ending up a little to the south-

Leipzig

east of Breslau when an armistice was declared on 4 June.

Hostilities between the main bodies actually ceased on the 2nd, but further afield the details were not received until as late as 9 June. This was the case with Bülow, still covering Berlin and now facing Oudinot. Oudinot's men had suffered the most at Bautzen and had been given a short period to reorganize before being sent off to menace the Prussian capital. Two actions were fought between the two generals, with Bülow having the advantage when news of the armistice halted all further activity.

Elsewhere, Davout and Vandamme were operating on the lower Elbe, taking Hamburg and Lubeck thanks to the inactivity of the Swedes in Mecklenberg. Further up the Elbe a Russian force observing Magdeburg surprised a raw division of Arrighi's newly-formed cavalry corps at Leipzig. The French were most fortunate in that the Russians were prevented from occupying the town by the terms of the ceasefire.

The armistice should not be thought of as a sudden and unexpected event. Negotiations for a

Connewitz

campaign. The players may indulge in negotiations as their historical counterparts did, but the outcome may be very different. It would be wrong for the umpire to impose an artificial ceasefire. On the other hand, Austria's entry into the war will call for some supervision. The umpire must inform the Austrian player of the state of his army as it is being built up and there should, perhaps, be some level, known only to the umpire, which will trigger an automatic declaration of war by Austria. Prior to this the umpire could periodically determine, on a random basis, whether Austria makes a premature entry. Obviously the odds will be low at the beginning of the campaign, increasing with the passage of time. The odds will have to be modified to take account of events. For example, the odds will be lowered for each French victory and increased with each French defeat. If the Allies get the upper hand early in the campaign it is natural to think that the Austrians will want to contribute some force, however weak, in order to secure a place at any subsequent peace conference.

Returning to historical fact, the Austrians actually declared war on 12 August, two days after the armistice had been denounced by the Allies. As with Prussia, the Austrian army had been limited by treaty; but although she was allowed 150,000 men, so bankrupt was the country after defeats in four previous campaigns that even this figure was not maintained. Annual training was shortened and the army kept on the lowest peace footing. The only full-strength corps available at the start of 1813 was that of Schwarzenberg, which had accompanied the *Grande Armée* into Russia. By the end of the armistice Austria was ready with a hastily trained field force of 194,000 and a further 27,500 troops in garrison. Of the field force, 66,000 were employed in other theatres, leaving 128,000 for the main Army of Bohemia.

There is one more aspect of the armistice to consider, and this is the manner of its termination. It was the convention of the time that notification, usually of about ten days, was given by any side intending to resume hostilities. This may seem a liability at times, but armistices have always been viewed with respect and the principle should be

general peace had been going on since the previous December when Napoleon returned from Russia. Austria was supposed to be acting as mediator, but the terms offered were quite impossible for Napoleon to accept. The armistice was concluded ostensibly as a step towards a peace conference, but the reality was that both sides merely wanted a period for reinforcement and resupply. Napoleon's agreement to the armistice has been the subject of much controversy, because it is generally recognized that the Allies had most to gain. This opinion, however, is given with the benefit of hindsight. At the time Napoleon could not know for certain that Austria would throw in her lot with the Allies. Even Bernadotte with his Swedes did not believe it likely. Even if he could have known, the Emperor still had pressing reasons for agreeing to an armistice. His young soldiers were desperately tired, and above all he needed to build up his cavalry arm.

The questions posed by the ceasefire demand careful consideration in the context of a wargames strictly adhered to, as should any other terms agreed. Blücher was universally condemned when he advanced on Breslau two days before the end of the 1813 armistice.

As we have seen, the ceasefire was arranged not as a prelude to peace but as a period of reorganization. Napoleon's arrangements for the future revolved, rather unusually for him, about a defensive plan. He stated that he would let the Allies make the first move and then take advantage of any mistakes they made. This frame of mind does not show the Emperor at his best, but, having decided to act on the defensive, the rest of his plans were sound enough. There were three possible lines of defence: the Rhine, the Saale and the Elbe. A defence of the Rhine would involve giving up too much ground and would place the Allies within striking distance of France. This in turn would require the employment of many valuable troops on garrison duties. The Saale was little more than a stream and easily crossed at most points. The Elbe, by contrast, had much to recommend it. It was no mean physical obstacle and the French held all the fortified passages, although only Magdeburg was really strong. Hamburg, Torgau, Wittenberg and Dresden needed much work, which was put in hand at once. Dresden was made the centre of operations, and defences were constructed on both sides of the river as a precaution against an Austrian attack from Bohemia. Work was far from finished when hostilities were resumed, but the fortresses had been made proof against all but a major attack. Dresden had been stuffed full of supplies to give a measure of independence from the depots in France. Maps were produced from careful surveys, and Napoleon rode over much of the ground himself.

Napoleon's final plan saw his main army occupying a defensive position along a line from Dresden in the west through Zittau to Leignitz in the east. Napoleon expected the main thrust to come from the Austrians in Bohemia against his centre at Zittau, but he also saw the possibility of an attack along the left, or west, bank of the Elbe against Dresden. The left wing of the army about Leignitz faced towards the east to counter the threat posed by the Army of Silesia under

Leipzig

Blücher. The actual disposition of the various corps was as follows: St Cyr, with l'Heritier's cavalry corps was at Dresden supported by Vandamme and Kellerman's cavalry corps at Bautzen; Zittau was held by Poniatowski, whose corps had been released by the Austrians during the armistice (it will be remembered that Schwarzenberg had carried these men into Galicia with him on the retreat from Russia); the main reserve was behind Poniatowski at Gorlitz and consisted of Victor's corps, Latour-Maubourg's cavalry corps and the Guard; Ney, Lauriston and Sebastiani's cavalry were at Leignitz with Marmont and Macdonald in support at Bunzlau. The forces at Leignitz and Bunzlau were intended to hold Blücher while the rest of the army crushed the Austrians. If the latter did not attack directly, but instead moved to join the Silesian Army, the French were to concentrate at Bunzlau. No thought was given to the possibility that the Silesian Army might move to join the Austrians in Bohemia, but in fact a large portion of this army did just that.

Napoleon's defensive posture at this time has been criticized, but he was afraid that if he struck at either the Austrians or the Army of Silesia they would merely retire before him and he would again be robbed of the decisive victory he needed. Nor did he intend just to sit still. As soon as the Allies made a mistake he would be quick to seize the opportunity. His arrangements for the northern part of the theatre can be criticized with more justification. He still cherished the idea of capturing Berlin, partly because he held a particular grudge against the Prussians and

against Bernadotte, who was helping to guard the Prussian capital with his Army of the North, and partly because he still hoped to put into effect his very first plan of relieving the garrison of Danzig. For this venture Oudinot, Bertrand, Reynier and Arrighi's cavalry were to advance from the Elbe on Berlin with 75,000 men, Oudinot to be in overall command. Davout with 40,000 men was to advance on Berlin at the same time from Hamburg. His approach would leave Oudinot's force free to carry on towards Stettin.

In the Allied camp a dozen plans had been

The Plates

Colour photography by Brian Monaghan from layouts arranged and created by Peter Gilder. Colour centrespread map by Christine Howes. The figures and equipment used to create these battle scenes are basic wargames items as produced by well-known figure manufacturers, and are used by Peter Gilder in his normal wargaming. For the purpose of these photographs, however, the bases have been concealed with flock.

Plate A shows French Imperial Guard artillery batteries in action, being visited by the Emperor.

Plate B shows Napoleon studying his maps the night before the battle—a three-dimensional re-creation of a famous painting.

Plate C shows a regiment of Austrian Uhlan cavalry before Leipzig, with Austrian staff officers in the foreground.

Plate D shows the lie of the land, and the major troop dispositions of the Allied and French armies around Leipzig on the morning of 18 October 1813. The 'bodies of troops' shown on the map are, of course, stylized representations, for obvious reasons of scale. The key numbers refer to the listing on page 25.

Plate E shows Murat leading in person one of the cavalry charges in the engagement at

Liebertwolkwitz on the afternoon of 14 October. The initial clash was with Russian cavalry and Cossacks under Count Pahlen, but the fighting escalated with the arrival of Prussian reserve cavalry from Kleist's command. Though ultimately inconclusive, this was the largest cavalry engagement of 1813, and saw Murat lead the last great charge of his life. Identifiable in the photograph are Red Lancers, Chasseurs and Dragoons of the Guard, and cuirassiers.

Plate F shows a clash in the streets of Möckern on the afternoon of 16 October between infantry of Marmont's French VI Corps and Yorck's Prussian 1st Corps. The fighting in Möckern raged backwards and forwards throughout the afternoon, with the Prussians finally making good their capture of the village. This was the most important of three main engagements that day, and Napoleon's defeat was serious in that it shut him in on the northern flank.

Plate G shows the premature explosion of the mined bridge over the Elster at about 1 p.m. on 18 October, which trapped between 10,000 and 15,000 French troops east of the river. It is thought that the mine was set off by a nervous corporal, who came under fire from enemy skirmishers while his colonel was absent seeking precise orders.

B

C

Lindenthal

44

Mockern

43

42

Gohlis

Mockau

41 40 39

17

Schönefeld

16 15

Lindenau

Reudnitz

18

LEIPZIG

Schönau

Plagwitz

19

3

1

Connewitz

4

2

Meusdorf

25

23

21

Lössnig

22

20

Dolitz

24

Dösen

Markkleeburg

D

38　Plaussig

Pösen

Portitz

Cleuden

Taucha

36　37　Mill　Plösitz

Panitsch

13

Sommerfeld

35

Paunsdorf

Sellerhausen

Alten

Mölkau

Engelsdorf

12

Hirschfeld

33

10

32　34

8 Kötteritz

Zuckelhausen

11

7

Klein Pössnau

Zweinaundorf

9

Probstheide

Holzhausen

26　27

KOLMBERG

30　31

Seyfartshayn

28　29

GALGENBERG

Liebertwolkwitz

Güldengossa

E

G

considered and certain principles evolved from them. The overall idea was for the armies of the North, Silesia, Poland and Bohemia to converge slowly on the main French body. If any of them were attacked by Napoleon in person they were to retire while the others continued to advance. The French lines of communication and any force subsidiary to the main army could be attacked if the advantage lay with the Allies but not otherwise. This rather cautious approach has been attributed to the influence of Bernadotte, but the Austrians were as much responsible. Only Blücher favoured a head-on clash with Napoleon, and one wonders whether the decision to transfer the greater part of his force to the Army of Bohemia was taken in order to remove any temptation the old fire-eater might have felt towards independent action.

In accordance with their overall strategy of attacking the enemy's flanks and avoiding the main body, it was decided that the Army of Bohemia should move against St Cyr at Dresden by the left bank of the Elbe, while the Army of Silesia attacked Ney and Lauriston at Leignitz

---

KEY TO MAPS OF LEIPZIG, Morning of 16 October and 12 a.m. 18 October 1813
See Plate D, and pages 33 and 35

French formations:

1. Lefol's division
2. VIII Corps (Poniatowski)—26th & 27th Polish divisions
3. IV Cavalry Corps (Kellerman)—two divisions
4. IX Corps (Angereau)—51st, 52nd & 53rd divisions
5. II Corps (Victor)—4th, 5th & 6th divisions
6. V Cavalry Corps (Pajol)—two divisions
7. Imperial Guard infantry—two Old and two Young Guard divisions
8. I Cavalry Corps (Latour-Maubourg)—two divisions
9. XI Corps (Macdonald)—31st, 35th, 36th & 39th (Baden-Hessian) divisions
10. Guard Cavalry—two divisions plus, with one cuirassier division in support
11. V Corps (Lauriston)—10th, 16th & 19th divisions
12. II Cavalry Corps (Sebastiani)—two divisions
13. VII Corps (Reynier)—14th, 24th & 32nd (Saxon) divisions
14. VI Corps (Marmont)—20th, 21st (Württemberg) & 22nd (Württemberg) divisions
15. III Corps (Souham)—8th, 9th & 11th divisons
16. III Cavalry Corps (Arrighi)—two divisions
17. Dombrowski's Polish division.
18. Mortier—two Young Guard divisions
19. IV Corps (Bertrand)—12th, 15th (Italian) & 38th (Württemberg) divisions

Allied formations:

20. Austrian III Corps (Gyulai)—two divisions plus 1st Light Division
21. Remnant of Austrian II Corps (Lederer)—one division
22. Austrian Reserve Corps (Hessen-Homburg)—two divisions, one of which grenadier
23. Austrian I Corps (Colloredo)—two divisions
24. Austrian Reserve Cavalry (Nostitz)—one division of heavy cavalry
25. Prussian II Corps (Kleist)—9th, 10th, 11th & 12th brigades
26. Russian II Corps (Eugen)—3rd & 4th divisions
27. Russian I Corps (Gortschakov)—5th & 14th divisions
28. Russian V Guard Corps (Constantine)—1st & 2nd Guard divisions plus one Prussian Guard brigade
29. Russian, Prussian and Austrian Guard Cavalry
30. Austrian IV Corps (Klenau)—two divisions
31. Zeithen's Prussian brigade
32. Doctorow's Russian Corps—6th & 12th divisions
33. Russian Advance Guard—13th & 16th divisions
34. Platow's Cossacks
35. Austrian 2nd Light Division (Buhna)
36. Prussian III Corps (Bülow)- 3rd, 4th, 5th & 6th brigades plus one heavy cavalry division
37. Winzingerode's Russian Corps—21st, 24th, 26th & 27th divisions
38. Swedish I Corps (Steding)—1st, 2nd & 3rd divisions
39. Russian VIII Corps (St Priest)—11th & 17th divisions plus one heavy cavalry division
40. Russian IX Corps (Alsusieff)—9th & 15th divisions
41. Russian X Corps (Kapsevitch)—8th & 22nd divisions
42. Russian IV Corps (Leiven)—7th & 18th divisions
43. Russian VII Corps (Neverowski)—10th & 25th divisions
44. Prussian I Corps (Yorck)—Advance Guard, 1st, 2nd, 7th & 8th brigades

from the direction of Breslau. The French Emperor noted the transfer of troops from Blücher's army into Bohemia and began to think about striking a decisive blow against the reduced Silesian force. An alternative was to catch the transferred troops as they marched between the two armies. He decided to wait to see if these men were going to join the Austrians in a major attack on his centre at Zittau, but when they kept marching westwards (for the attack on Dresden) he determined to make his attempt against Blücher, using the left wing of his army supported by the Guard. Blücher dutifully retired before him and Napoleon followed until news reached him of the Austrian move against Dresden. He ordered Macdonald with his own corps and those of Ney and Lauriston to remain observing Blücher's army while he rushed back to Dresden with the Guard. Ney was senior to Macdonald, so he was ordered to headquarters to avoid any problems there. Souham, a divisional commander, was put in charge of Ney's corps. Unfortunately, these orders did not reach Ney, and for some reason he retired on Bunzlau with his entire corps—out of supporting distance of Macdonald.

At Dresden the Russians and Prussians transferred from the Army of Silesia were forcing St Cyr's men back on the town. On 25 August Schwarzenberg could have taken Dresden with these troops, but he decided to wait until his own Austrians were up. He was unaware that Napoleon was fast approaching with reinforcements. The Emperor wanted to cross the Elbe above Dresden and to attack Schwarzenberg's line of communication, but he was afraid for the safety of his great depot, and instead made directly for the Saxon capital. News was also coming in of a setback to Oudinot in the north which threatened to expose Napoleon's army to a flank attack from that direction. He was obliged to detach l'Heritier's cavalry from St Cyr to guard against this possibility, weakening the Dresden defences still further. These factors determined Napoleon to abandon an attempt at a *maneouvre sur les derrières* with his entire force, and he sent Vandamme alone to cross at Pirna. If he had instead sent Vandamme to reinforce St Cyr it is probable that Dresden

could have held out long enough for Napoleon to have realized his ambition and to have had the Army of Bohemia completely at his mercy.

The Battle of Dresden
26–27 August 1813

There is little from the wargaming aspect that can be learnt from the battle of Dresden. From the start the Allied dispositions were faulty. Bianchi was on the left facing an *ad hoc* force of elements of St Cyr's and Vandamme's corps under the command of Murat. He was separated from the rest of the army by the River Weisseritz, which was difficult to cross at the best of times except by a single bridge at Plauen. The weather during the battle was very bad and the small river became so swollen as to be completely impassable. It was expected that Bianchi would be reinforced by Klenau, but this officer failed to arrive in time. Bianchi had little of either cavalry or artillery, the only two arms of much use in wet weather, whereas Murat had the whole of Latour-Maubourg's cavalry corps by the second day, and plenty of guns. Murat launched an enveloping attack which drove the Austrians into the river, almost annihilating Bianchi's corps. The Allied cavalry was massed in the centre under the direct command of Schwarzenberg. Here they faced a network of earthworks, redoubts, walls and hedges which rendered them entirely useless. The French centre, under St Cyr, stayed on the defensive throughout the battle. Wittgenstein had charge of the Russians and Prussians on the right of the Allied line. His attack, along a course parallel to the Elbe, was severely hampered by enfilade fire from French artillery on the other side of the river. When his men had exhausted themselves against the French defenders, Napoleon launched an enveloping attack similar to the one Murat developed on the other wing. So, from a small bridgehead with 120,000 men, Napoleon succeeded in enveloping both flanks of an army 170,000 strong and inflicting a very severe defeat on them. The Allies lost about 35,000 men to the French losses of 10,000. When looking for the real cause of the French victory one need search no further than the person of Napoleon himself. It was his personality and his

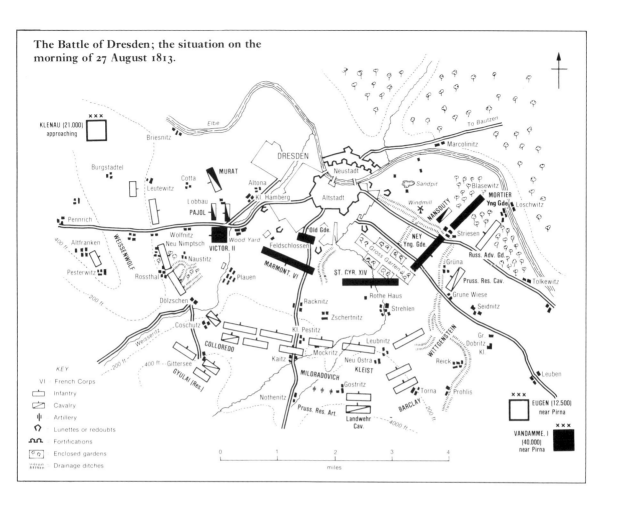

The Battle of Dresden; the situation on the morning of 27 August 1813.

KLENAU (21.000) approaching

Elbe

Briesnitz

To Bautzen

Burgstadtel

Marcolinitz

DRESDEN

MURAT

Cotta

Altona

Neustadt

Sandpit

Blasewitz

MORTIER
Yng Gde

Leutewitz

Kl Hamberg

Altstadt

Windmill

NANSOUTY

Loschwitz

Lobbau

PAJOL

Pennrich

Old Gde.

NEY
Yng. Gde.

Striesen

Russ. Adv. Gd.

Wolfnitz

WEISSENWOLF

Altfranken

Neu Nimptsch

Wood Yard

VICTOR. II

Feldschlossen

Gross Garten

Grüna

Naustitz

Pesterwitz

Rossthal

MARMONT. VI

ST. CYR. XIV

Pruss. Res. Cav.

Tolkewitz

Plauen

Grune Wiese

Dölzschen

Racknitz

Rothe Haus

Seidnitz

Zschertnitz

Strehlen

Coschutz

Gr.
Dobritz
Kl.

COLLOREDO

Kl. Pestitz

Leubnitz

WITTGENSTEIN

Reick

Leuben

GYULAI (Res.)

Gittersee

Kaitz

Mockritz

Neu Ostra

KLEIST

MILORADOVICH

Gostritz

Torna

Prohlis

EUGEN (12.500)
near Pirna

Nothenitz

Pruss. Res. Art.

BARCLAY

Landwehr
Cav.

VANDAMME, I
(40.000)
near Pirna

KEY

VI   French Corps
      Infantry
      Cavalry
      Artillery
      Lunettes or redoubts
      Fortifications
      Enclosed gardens
      Drainage ditches

0   1   2   3   4

miles

will that won the battle of Dresden. For that brief moment he was once again the Napoleon of earlier years.

The Allies went into council once more, and agreed that a retreat was the only course open to them. It took Napoleon some time on the 28th to realize that his enemy were retreating, but he quickly organized the pursuit. There was a lot of confusion on both sides, however, which turned out to the Allies' advantage. Murat's success on the eastern flank robbed the Allies of the use of the one good road back into Bohemia on that side, while on the other side Vandamme, crossing at Pirna as planned, had easily overcome the observing force placed there under Eugen of Württemberg and cut the only other good road. The Allies were forced to struggle through the mud of very inferior roads towards the mountain passes back into Bohemia. It only required Napoleon to send a good part of his army after

Vandamme along the good road into Bohemia for the Allies to be trapped before they could debouch from the passes on the poor routes they were being forced to take. Unhappily for the French, a movement by Barclay de Tolly's corps from one of these roads to another further west convinced Napoleon that the whole Allied army was not trying to retreat through the mountain passes directly to the south, but was instead heading south-west. He accordingly switched the emphasis of the pursuit over to Murat's wing. Vandamme was to continue alone and to destroy Eugen's force which was still travelling south, fighting rearguard actions all along the way. The last of these was at Külm, and Vandamme's men were thrown back by the severity of it. When Vandamme renewed the attack on the next day, 30 August, the Allies had been reinforced to some 44,000 men against Vandamme's 32,000. The battle was going neither one way nor the other

27

French 12-pounder gun and 6-inch howitzer of the Gribeauval system. The excellent Gribeauval system comprised a range of 4-pounder, 8-pounder and 12-pounder cannons and 6-inch and 8-inch howitzers. Dating originally from 1776, the range featured a standardized carriage with many interchangeable parts, elevating screws and calibrated sights. (Richard Scollins)

until at 11 a.m. Kleist's corps suddenly appeared in the rear of the French. He had been ordered to join Eugen's troops south of the mountains, but found that the passes on the roads he was using were blocked. The only possibility left to him was to follow the road along which Vandamme had travelled and to cut his way through that general's corps. In the end it was Vandamme's men who had to cut their way back through the Prussians.

At the battle of Külm Vandamme was captured and half of his corps destroyed. Napoleon himself must take the blame for this disaster. He assumed in the first place, on quite insufficient information, that the enemy were not falling back directly on the mountain passes and, when he discovered his mistake on the afternoon of the 29th, he failed to send any support to Vandamme until eight hours later. Mortier with two Guard divisions was available within supporting distance of Vandamme, and if he had been sent immediately the battle would have had a different outcome. St Cyr, who had been following Kleist, should perhaps

carry some of the blame in that he allowed the Prussians to conduct a march across the front of the French unmolested. What had happened was that St Cyr had found himself wandering into the area assigned to Marmont and, fearful of the confusion this situation could bring about, had halted to await orders from Napoleon.

The entire episode emphasizes the importance of reconnaissance, an area of wargaming for which the umpire must bear responsibility. The players may assign their cavalry patrols, but only the umpire will be in a position to know what they discover. He must use his judgement in providing the players with information and they must bear the responsibility for interpreting it.

Vandamme's loss was not the only disaster that befell the French at this time. Oudinot's project against Berlin failed, and to the east Macdonald was overwhelmed by the Army of Silesia. The affair between Macdonald and Blücher was a messy one. Macdonald had been ordered to drive the Silesian Army back to Jauer, about ten miles south-east of Leignitz, and then to fall back twenty miles or so to the River Bobr and adopt a defensive posture. Napoleon estimated that Blücher, when he resumed the offensive, would make for a number of targets, whereupon Macdonald should concentrate his force and defeat the enemy in detail. Having more or less attained the first part of his task Macdonald continued on the offensive contrary to the Emperor's instructions. Blücher, meanwhile, had realized that Napoleon was no longer with the forces facing him and, thinking the French would go on the defensive as they should have done, he decided to attack himself. The two advancing armies met each other, much to the surprise of both, on 26 August along the River Katzbach— from which the ensuing battle took its name. The weather was as bad as that at Dresden, and the men were reduced to using their bayonets and musket butts in a confused affair which saw the French thoroughly beaten. The French at first had only the corps of Macdonald and Lauriston, about 56,000 men, because Ney had marched off to Bunzlau with his troops as described earlier. When these eventually arrived, now under the command of Souham as Napoleon ordered,

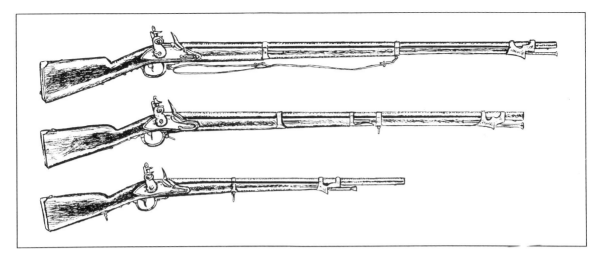

French infantry musket, dragoon musket, and cavalry carbine. Muskets of the period were essentially similar in all armies. The typical infantry weapon had a 42-inch-long smooth-bore barrel with a calibre of about .75 of an inch. The overall length was about five feet, with an 18-inch bayonet fitting to the muzzle with a ring socket. The range was around 200 yards, but accuracy dropped off so badly over 100 yards that normal combat firing ranges were usually well within the latter figure. It has been calculated that in battle only two or three per cent of all rounds fired were effective; but the discharge of the first few volleys against closely ordered troops at close range could be devastating. After a dozen rounds at most, barrels began to foul up badly and flints became damaged, and harried infantrymen tended to start making mistakes—the most serious of those commonly reported were the firing away of the ramrod, and the inadvertent double or triple loading of a musket before firing, with explosive results. (Richard Scollins)

Macdonald had some 88,000 against Blücher's 90,000. In the battle the Prussian and Russian cavalry proved themselves better than Sebastiani's troops, which showed that the French cavalry were still qualitatively poor. Macdonald lost 15,000 men and the rest scrambled back behind the Bobr.

On 18 August, Oudinot was at Baruth about three marches south of Berlin. From here he took his own corps and those of Bertrand and Reynier to Luckenwalde before turning north to Berlin. He reached Trebbin, twenty-five miles south of Berlin, on the 22nd. From here he had to pass through very close country and was forced to march his three corps along widely separated roads with poor lateral communications. Oudinot's corps was on the left, Reynier in the centre and Bertrand on the right. Oudinot moved rather slowly and had not succeeded in debouching from this difficult country by the end of the day. Bertrand on the right came up against Tauenzien's men and was brought to a halt. He did not press the attack because he thought the Prussians were bound to retire as the other two French corps advanced out of the forest. In fact only Reynier

managed this, and he found himself up against the strongest of the Prussian corps under Bülow about the village of Gross Beeren. Here again the rain prevented the use of infantry firepower and the French, who seem to have been low on morale, were beaten back. Losses were not heavy, but a dispirited Oudinot withdrew his entire force back to its starting point. Without a doubt the Prussian countryside was very hostile to the French, and this should be reflected in any morale rules which are used in the campaign. There was no other reason why Oudinot should have given up his task. His retreat, of course, forced Davout to give up as well, and he returned to Hamburg. The only other point to note from this affair was Bernadotte's refusal to commit his Swedes against Oudinot's corps. He believed Oudinot to be far stronger than he actually was.

We now see Napoleon at his worst. Up to this point he had regarded the Army of Bohemia as his principal objective. Suddenly he lost all interest in it and instead considered two other schemes. The first, a drive on Prague, he rejected as being of little value, but in the second he returned to the idea of a major push towards Berlin and thence to Stettin, leaving only a defending force about Dresden. Events overtook him, however, and he found himself obliged to go to the relief of Macdonald, whose forces facing Blücher were rapidly disintegrating. Having driven Blücher back once more, he had to rush back to Dresden where it seemed likely that the Bohemian army was about to make another attempt on the town. The outcome of all this was that only Oudinot's original force was available for another attempt on Berlin. This time Ney was put in command.

The plan was for Ney to take his three corps from Wittenberg east to Luckau where Napoleon would have had another 25,000 men but for the distractions already mentioned. From there the whole force of about 80,000 would make for Berlin. Oudinot was to lead the movement out of Wittenberg with Bertrand following. Reynier was to go first north and then to turn right, acting as flank guard to the other two corps. Against this movement Bernadotte intended for Tauenzien to hold up the French with 10,000 men, falling back on the rest of his corps at Dennewitz, while Bülow, Winzingerode and Steding worked around the rear of the enemy. Tauenzien's advance guard was duly pushed back and then Ney ordered Oudinot to halt until Reynier completed his turn to the right. Bertrand was to act as flank guard covering this manoeuvre, so he advanced towards Tauenzien at Dennewitz. Ney had no intention of fighting a battle on this day, 6 September, but Bertrand launched himself into one just the same. His men were overthrown by the appearance of Bülow on the left, but the situation righted itself when Reynier came up after having travelled along the wrong road. This piece of misdirection meant that Oudinot waited in vain for Reynier's appearance and it was only in the afternoon that Ney ordered him to Dennewitz. The situation at the time of Oudinot's arrival was that Bülow's left was making ground, but his right was in some danger. Winzingerode and Steding were coming up from that direction but Bülow would need to hold on a while longer yet. Fortunately for him, Ney had fallen victim to his frequent habit of acting the rôle of corps instead of army com-

One type of French supply train waggon. (Richard Scollins)

mander. At the moment his attention was engaged with Bülow's successful left wing and he ordered Oudinot across to this side of the battlefield. Oudinot was able to see that an opportunity was being missed to roll Bülow's corps up from their right, or at least to separate them from Bernadotte, but he said nothing out of spite at being superseded in command by Ney. As the Russians and Swedes began to arrive the French broke in panic, Oudinot and Reynier going back to Torgau and Bertrand, with Ney, to Dahme and from thence to Torgau as well, being severely cut up again in the process. Altogether Ney lost 22,000 men to the Allies' 10,000.

Napoleon received news of this later disaster with outward calm. Perhaps he was already a beaten man and resigned to it. He was then at Dresden, it will be remembered, to deal with a new threat from the Army of Bohemia. In fact this was merely a demonstration to give Blücher another chance at finishing Macdonald off, but it was a very dangerous one. Schwarzenberg had divided his force for an advance along both sides of the Elbe, an opportunity which the old Napoleon would never have missed. He was content to chase off those troops on the left bank but left it at that. Schwarzenberg realized his error and reunited his army on the left bank of the Elbe.

Elsewhere the flying columns of Cossack raiders were achieving spectacular, if strategically unimportant, successes, all of which helped to sap the French morale. Napoleon decided to withdraw all his army behind the Elbe. He was on the defensive and the end was in sight.

As September passed into October, Napoleon

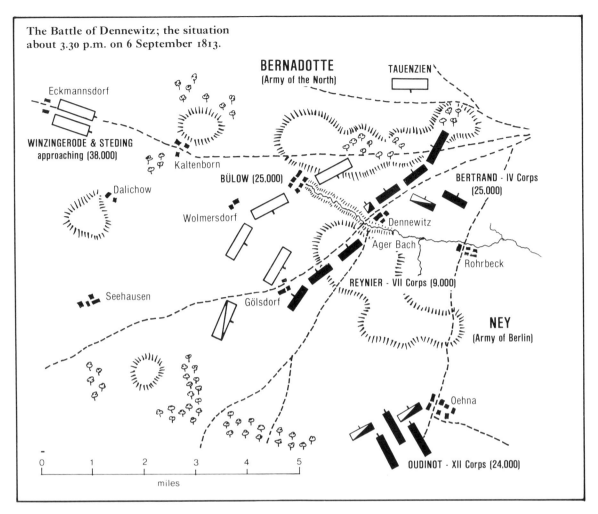

The Battle of Dennewitz; the situation about 3.30 p.m. on 6 September 1813.

BERNADOTTE
(Army of the North)

TAUENZIEN

Eckmannsdorf

WINZINGERODE & STEDING
approaching (38,000)

Kaltenborn

BÜLOW (25,000)

BERTRAND - IV Corps
(25,000)

Dalichow

Wolmersdorf

Dennewitz

Ager Bach

Rohrbeck

Seehausen

Gölsdorf

REYNIER - VII Corps (9,000)

NEY
(Army of Berlin)

Oehna

OUDINOT - XII Corps (24,000)

0   1   2   3   4   5

miles

was obliged to send his marshals hither and thither on each new report of the enemy's doings. In truth the Allied plans lacked any firm direction, but it was decided that the Army of Bohemia should switch its attention from Dresden to Leipzig. The Army of Poland under Bennigsen, coming up from the east towards the position on the Elbe occupied by Blücher, would instead swing south-west to join Schwarzenberg's men. Blücher covered this flank march and then, with Bernadotte, crossed the Elbe and made for the Mulde.

With the Allies thus divided, Napoleon, in the centre, determined to deal with Blücher and Bernadotte before turning on Schwarzenberg. Murat was sent off to Freiburg with the corps of Victor, Lauriston and Poniatowski and the cavalry corps of l'Heritier, now commanded by Milhaud. Arrighi was to garrison Leipzig, and

Dresden was protected by St Cyr and Lobau (Vandamme's replacement). At one point Napoleon thought to abandon Dresden as worthless. The two corps tied up there would have been very useful at Leipzig. For the venture against Blücher, believed to be at Duben, Napoleon took the corps of Souham, Marmont, Macdonald, Bertrand, Reynier and the Guard along with the cavalry corps of Sebastiani and Latour-Maubourg: 120,000 men in all. Blücher, not without difficulty, managed to avoid this blow and persuaded a shaky Bernadotte, who was safely to the north at Dessau, to move westwards on the Saale instead of back to the Elbe. This was an unusual decision which left communications with Berlin threatened. Nevertheless, Blücher remained resolutely near Halle until Schwarzenberg's army came up to Leipzig. On 14 October the cavalry of the latter had fought a

Leipzig

very large battle with Murat's cavalry at Leibert-wolkwitz, south-east of Leipzig. It had been inconclusive, but Murat could less well afford to lose men than the Allies.

By now Napoleon had realized that his plans had come to nothing and that his whole army would have to retire on Leipzig for a major battle. By nightfall on the 14th, 140,000 French troops were about Leipzig. Another 20,000 would arrive over the next two days. To the south they faced Schwarzenberg's 120,000 with Bennigsen's 24,000 fast approaching. Some of the Austrians had crossed to the west of the River Pleisse, causing Napoleon to think that Blücher and Bernadotte had somehow slipped around the French flank to join Schwarzenberg. In fact Blücher with his 82,000 men was a few miles to the north-west with a reluctant Bernadotte tagging along in the rear with another 71,000. Had Napoleon been aware of this his arrangements would have been very different.

The Battle of Leipzig
16–19 October 1813
On 15 October both sides moved to take up their positions. The battlefield of Leipzig can conveniently be divided into sectors with the town itself at the centre. The rivers Elster and Pleisse run side by side up from the south, passing between Leipzig and the village of Lindenau before turning west to join the Saale. The area between the two rivers is of a marshy nature, barely passable to troops. Leipzig is linked to Lindenau by a wood-and-stone causeway, and from there three roads go to the west, south-west and south. It was along the first two of these that the French eventually retreated to Weissenfels. Note that Napoleon arrived at Leipzig from

Duben to the north-east and that he considered this direction, back towards the Elbe, to be his line of operations. His forced retreat in the opposite direction meant the abandonment of great quantities of baggage and material. It would have been Bernadotte's task to block this alternative had he not been marching so far behind Blücher. As it was, only the Austrian corps of Gyulai from the Army of Bohemia was sent across the two rivers against Lindenau. The village was at first held only by a part of the Leipzig garrison under Arrighi, who had been made governor earlier in the campaign. He probably had about 5,000 infantry and his cavalry corps of 3,000. When Gyulai made his attack Bertrand was sent to help, quite unnecessarily, with his entire corps.

The northern part of the battlefield was Ney's responsibility. It is delineated by the Elster and Pleisse, running west from Leipzig, and the road to Wurzen and Dresden, running east. Napoleon was not expecting a serious threat from this direction and Ney had only the corps of Bertrand, Marmont, Souham and Reynier as well as the Leipzig garrison. Napoleon intended that either Bertrand or Marmont should be drawn later to the southern sector, but, as we have seen, Bertrand was thrown into Lindenau. Marmont had begun to march as the Army of Silesia arrived on Ney's front. Ney ordered Marmont back into line again and Napoleon was unable to complete his scheme for the southern sector of the battlefield.

The area to the south-east of Leipzig, between the Pleisse and the road to Dresden, is best described as a series of low ridges running out from Leipzig like the spokes of a wheel. There were numerous villages scattered about, as indeed there were over the whole battlefield. Here Napoleon faced the Army of Bohemia, and he had no intention of fighting a purely defensive battle. Murat, with his right against the Pleisse, was to pin Schwarzenberg's men with the corps of Poniatowski, Lauriston and Victor, while on the left, Macdonald, with Sebastiani's cavalry and either Bertrand or Marmont, would turn the Allied right as Ney had done at Bautzen. At this point Augereau (brought up from the Saale where he had been guarding the French rear), the

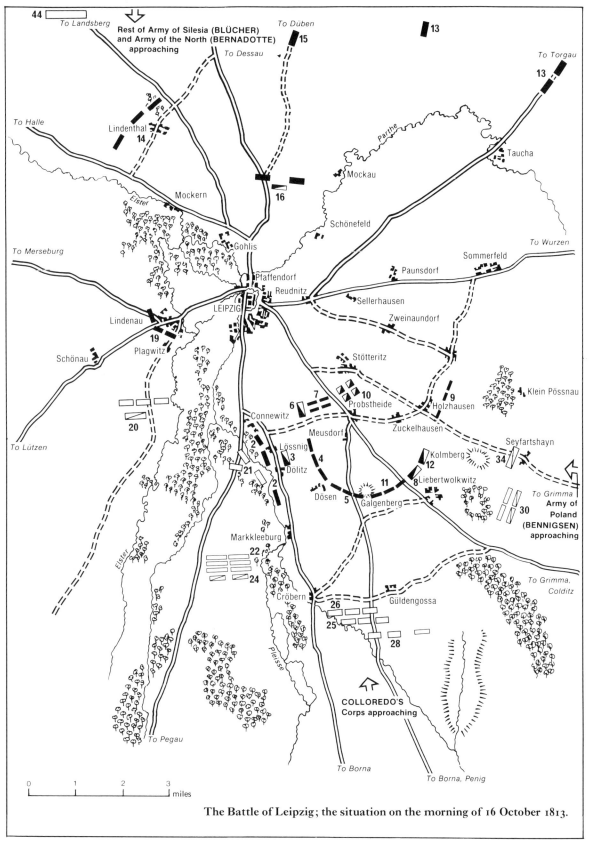

The Battle of Leipzig; the situation on the morning of 16 October 1813.

Guard and the cavalry of Kellerman and Milhaud would be hurled at the weakened Allied line.

Bertrand and Marmont were, of course, not destined to appear. Ney did send Souham in their place, but, under pressure from Blücher, recalled them before again changing his mind. Souham never did arrive on the southern sector and Napoleon tried to implement his plan without further aid. Macdonald began to push the Allies back on his wing, but insufficient strength caused him to fail in turning their flank as Napoleon wanted. The Emperor tried a frontal assault, bringing Augereau, the Guard and all the cavalry into the line, but he only succeeded in pushing the Allies back from the gains they had made.

Schwarzenberg's plan lacked subtlety. The Allies were to make a head-on attack while Gyulai assaulted Lindenau across the Pleisse and Elster, and Meerveldt's Austrians struggled up between the two rivers to turn Murat's right. Gyulai was easily beaten back by Bertrand, and Meerveldt was pinned down by intelligently applied artillery fire. Schwarzenberg had originally wanted this attempt on the French flank to be undertaken by a much larger force but had been overruled by the Czar, probably wisely. The frontal assault had at first succeeded, but all the ground gained was lost when Napoleon made his counter-attack.

All of this happened on the first day of the battle. On the 17th, little was done by either side as both revised their plans. By now Napoleon knew that Blücher was about to be joined by Bernadotte and Schwarzenberg by Bennigsen. His retreat to the Elbe was being cut off, but he could still take the greater part of his army safely away by Weissenfels via Lindenau. He is universally condemned for not doing so. He had no room left on the battlefield for manoeuvre, and the Allies, with their vastly superior strength, had no need for it. Bennigsen came up on Schwarzenberg's left and Bernadotte on Blücher's so that the two new arrivals linked about Taucha on the Dresden road. Without allowing for casualties, Napoleon had brought on to the battlefield 157,000 men and 900 guns against the Allies' 287,000 and 1,500 guns. The French did not collapse in panic on the 18th and fought desperately as they were forced back, village by village, on Leipzig, but the end was clearly in sight.

There remains the question of why Schwarzenberg permitted the road to Weissenfels to remain open. Did this have anything to do with the Austrians' wish not to have Napoleon totally destroyed? We can only wonder. In the early hours of the 19th Napoleon began his retreat. The campaign was over.

Impression of the French retreat after Leipzig, with Napoleon in centre foreground preceded by *Chasseurs à cheval* **of the Guard; in the background the Elster bridge is blown.**

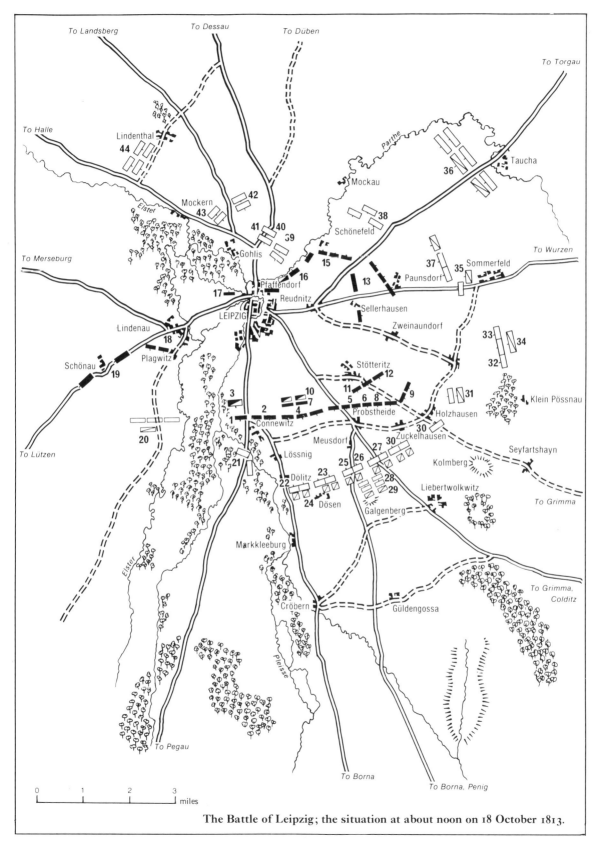

The Battle of Leipzig; the situation at about noon on 18 October 1813.

To Landsberg

To Dessau

To Düben

To Torgau

To Halle

Lindenthal
44

Parthe

36

Taucha

Mockau

42

Mockern
43

41 **40**
39

Gohlis

Schönefeld
38

To Merseburg

To Wurzen

Pfaffendorf
16

37

Paunsdorf

35 Sommerfeld

17 Reudnitz

15

13

LEIPZIG

Sellerhausen

Lindenau

Zweinaundorf

18

33

34

Schönau

Plagwitz

32

19

Stötteritz
12

Klein Pössnau

3

10
7

11

5 **6** **8** **9**

31

2 **4**

Probstheide

Holzhausen

1

Connewitz

30

Zuckelhausen

20

Meusdorf

27 **30**

Seyfartshayn

21

Lössnig

25 **26**

Kolmberg

28

Dölitz **23**

22

24 Dösen

29

Liebertwolkwitz

To Grimma

Galgenberg

To Lützen

Markkleeburg

Cröbern

Güldengossa

To Grimma,
Colditz

To Pegau

To Borna

To Borna, Penig

0   1   2   3
|____|____|____|____| miles

35

The following tables are taken from contemporary accounts. The discrepancies in the totals must be assumed to arise from the inclusion of artillery crews, engineers, and so on.

FRENCH CORPS STRENGTHS
April to October 1813

Corps	Commander	April	May			August
		Total strength	*infantry*	*cavalry*	*guns*	*Total strength*
I	Vandamme					
	(later Lobau)	—	—	—	—	32,000
II	Victor	—	13,000	—	16	21,000
III	Ney					
	(later Souham)	45,000	27,000	1,200	140	32,000
IV	Bertrand	30,000	23,500	600	60	21,000
V	Lauriston	22,000	25,000	—	140	35,000
VI	Marmont	25,000	20,000	600	120	30,000
VII	Reynier	—	9,500	150	—	12,000
VIII	Poniatowski	(held in Galicia by the Austrians—9,000)				8,000
IX	Augereau	—	—	—	—	10,000
X	Rapp	(besieged in Danzig—8,000)				
XI	Macdonald	22,000	15,500	300	90	21,000
XII	Oudinot	25,000	23,000	—	80	24,000
XIII	Davout	18,000	20,000	2,000	70	37,000
XIV	St Cyr	—	—	—	—	20,000
1st Cavalry Corps	Latour-Maubourg	4,000	—	9,800	30	10,000
2nd Cavalry Corps	Sebastiani	—	—	—	—	10,000
3rd Cavalry Corps	Arrighi	—	—	—	—	10,000
4th Cavalry Corps	Kellerman	—	—	—	—	5,000
5th Cavalry Corps	l'Heritier					
	(later Milhaud)	—	—	—	—	5,000
Old Guard		3,000	4,000	—	} 110	7,000
Young Guard		8,000	13,500	—		32,000
Guard Cavalry	Nansouty	4,000	—	4,000	20	10,000

Note: the Corps shown as not having been constituted in April and May were in the process of being built up. They were at approximately divisional strength during this period.

Barn outside Leipzig

Richer Gardens, Leipzig

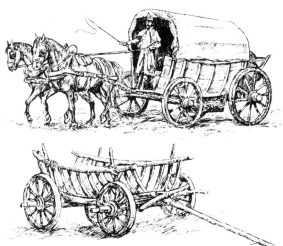

Typical varieties of French supply waggons. Napoleon's capability to supply his armies for short periods of very rapid movement often contributed to his success as a strategist, but the French were no more able to sustain long campaigns without proper lines of supply than were any of the other armies of the day. It often proved possible to live off the land for short, sometimes decisive periods, but only high morale enabled soldiers to withstand the privations inseparable from these campaign conditions. (Richard Scollins)

ALLIED CORPS STRENGTHS

April and May 1813

Commander	Corps Nationality	April			May		
		infantry	*cavalry*	*guns*	*infantry*	*cavalry*	*guns*
Barclay de Tolly	Russian	10,000	4,000	84	9,100	3,000	84
Berg							
(Gortchakov)	Russian	6,200	900	60	10,000	2,400	66
Blücher	Prussian	18,500	5,500	92	17,000	4,700	90
Bülow	Prussian	22,000	5,500	120	21,500	6,500	120
Kleist	Prussian/Russian	4,000	1,800	48	3,700	1,300	40
Miloradovich							
(Constantine)	Russian	5,000	2,750	86	8,800	5,200	54
Tormassov	Russian*	9,600	5,200	136	11,300	5,350	252
Winzingerode	Russian	6,400	6,700	90	6,400	6,700	90
Yorck	Prussian	6,500	1,300	40	4,120	1,210	36

* Russian reserve, including the Guard.

Note: the allied strengths at the end of the armistice in August can be regarded as similar to those given in the order of battle for Leipzig. Although heavy losses had been incurred at Dresden, and to a lesser extent at Kulm, the Katzbach and Gross Beeren, these had more or less been replaced by mid-October, whereas Napoleon received few reinforcements after August.

FRENCH CORPS STRENGTHS
at Leipzig, 17 October 1813

Position	Corps	Commander	Infantry	Cavalry	Total
Extreme right:	IV	Bertrand	15,000		15,000 foot
Right (Murat):	VIII	Poniatowski	8,000		8,000
	II	Victor	16,000		16,000
	4th Cavalry	Kellerman		3,000	3,000
					39,000 foot, 3,000 horse
Centre:	IX	Augereau	10,000		10,000
	V	Lauriston	9,000		9,000
	XI	Macdonald	15,000		15,000
	1st Cavalry	Latour-Maubourg		4,500	4,500
	2nd Cavalry	Sebastiani		4,800	4,800
	5th Cavalry	Milhaud		3,000	3,000
					34,000 foot, 12,300 horse
Left (Ney):	VI	Marmont	18,000		18,000
	III	Souham	15,000		15,000
	VII	Reynier	8,000		8,000
	3rd Cavalry	Arrighi		3,000	3,000
					41,000 foot, 3,000 horse
Reserve:	Old Guard		4,000		4,000
	Young Guard		16,000		16,000
	Cavalry	Nansouty		4,800	4,800
					20,000 foot, 4,800 horse
				Grand total:	134,000 foot, 23,100 horse
					157,100 men

Not present:
I Corps, Lobau, at Dresden
X Corps, Rapp, at Danzig
XIII Corps, Davout, at Hamburg
XIV Corps, St Cyr, at Dresden

Grimma Gate, Leipzig

A French field forge. (Richard Scollins)

ALLIED CORPS STRENGTHS
at Leipzig, 17 October 1813

The Great Army:

Austrians (Schwarzenberg):	Advanced Guard (Liechtenstein)	2,000 foot	1,600 horse
	1st Corps (Colloredo)	9,000	1,200
	2nd Corps (Meerveldt)	6,000	1,000
	3rd Corps (Gyulai)	7,000	1,500
	4th Corps (Klenau)	9,000	2,000
	Reserve (Hesse-Hombourg)	6,000	3,500
		39,000 foot	10,800 horse
Principal Corps (Barclay):	Russian 1st Corps (Wittgenstein)	8,000	
	Russian 2nd Corps (Eugen)	8,000	
	Prussian 2nd Corps (Kleist)	24,000	5,000
		40,000 foot	5,000 horse
Reserve (Constantine):	Russian 3rd Grenadier Corps (Rajevsky)	8,000	
	Russian 5th Guards Corps (Yermolov)	10,000	
	Austrian, Russian and Prussian Cavalry (Galitzin)		8,000
		18,000 foot	8,000 horse

continued overleaf

continued from previous page

Army of Silesia (Blücher) :

Russians (Langeron):	6th Corps (Czerbatov)	8,000 foot	
	8th Corps (St Priest)	8,000	
	9th Corps (Alsusiev)	8,000	
	10th Corps (Kapsevitch)	8,000	
	Cavalry (Korf)		5,000
		32,000 foot	5,000 horse
Russians (Sacken):	4th Corps (Lieven)	6,000	
	7th Corps (Neverovski)	6,000	
	Cavalry (Vassiltchikoff)		3,000
		12,000 foot	3,000 horse
Prussians (Yorck):	1st Corps	25,000 foot	5,000 horse

Army of the North :

Prussian 3rd Corps (Bülow)	20,000	4,000
Swedish Corps (Steding)	18,000	2,000
Russian Corps (Winzingerode)	14,000	3,000
	64,000 foot	9,000 horse

Detachments from Army of Poland :

Russian and Austrian troops (Benningsen)	20,000 foot	4,000 horse
Grand total:	250,000 foot	49,800 horse
	299,800 men	